DEVILS TOWER

By Roman Harasymiw

Gareth Stevens
PUBLISHING

Please visit our website, www.garethstevens.com. For a free color catalog of all our high-quality books, call toll free 1-800-542-2595 or fax 1-877-542-2596.

Library of Congress Cataloging-in-Publication Data

Harasymiw, Roman.
Devils Tower / by Roman Harasymiw.
 p. cm. — (Scariest places on Earth)
Includes index.
ISBN 978-1-4824-1152-2 (pbk.)
ISBN 978-1-4824-1153-9 (6-pack)
ISBN 978-1-4824-1151-5 (library binding)
1. Devils Tower National Monument (Wyo.) — Juvenile literature. I. Title.
F767.D47 H37 2015
978.7—d23

First Edition

Published in 2015 by
Gareth Stevens Publishing
111 East 14th Street, Suite 349
New York, NY 10003

Designer: Katelyn E. Reynolds
Editor: Therese Shea

Photo credits: Cover, p. 1 Kathyrn Froilan/Flickr/Getty Images; cover, pp. 1–24 (background texture) Eky Studio/Shutterstock.com; cover, pp. 1–24 (creepy design elements) Dmitry Natashin/Shutterstock.com; p. 5 (image) John_Brueske/iStock/Thinkstock.com; p. 5 (map) Uwe Dedering/Wikipedia.com; p. 6 Eric Isselee/Shutterstock.com; p. 7 Jason Patrick Ross/Shutterstock.com; p. 9 (sign) Ildar Sagdejev/Wikipedia.com; p. 9 (Devils Tower) gnagel/iStock/Thinkstock.com; p. 11 Images Etc Ltd/Stockbyte/Getty Images; p. 13 (lava inset) rz_design/iStock/Thinkstock.com; p. 13 (main) Steven Prorak/iStock/Thinkstock.com; p. 14 Dave White/iStock/Thinkstock.com; p. 15 (top) crash1965/iStock/Thinkstock.com; p. 15 (bottom) Steven Cooper/iStock/Thinkstock.com; p. 16 Hulton Archive/Getty Images; p. 17 MyLoupe/Universal Images Group/Getty Images; p. 19 Keith Ladzinski/Aurora/Getty Images; p. 21 CrackerClips/iStock/Thinkstock.com.

Printed in the United States of America

CPSIA compliance information: Batch #CS15GS: For further information contact Gareth Stevens, New York, New York at 1-800-542-2595.

CONTENTS

Words in the glossary appear in **bold** type the first time they are used in the text.

SOMETHING'S WEIRD IN WYOMING

Devils Tower may sound like a scary amusement park ride, but it's been around for a lot longer than any amusement park. It's actually a rock formation in northeastern Wyoming that rises 867 feet (264 m) from its base to its summit, or top. It has a flat summit, which makes it look strange and unlike most mountains you might see.

Devils Tower is a site unlike any other, which is why it gets many visitors. But how did it get that frightening name?

Wyoming

Devils Tower rises 1,267 feet (386 m) above the nearby Belle Fourche (FOOSH) River.

A KIOWA TALE

Native Americans were the first to set eyes on Devils Tower's amazing height and shape. They passed down several **legends** about how it formed.

A story from the Kiowa tribe tells of seven little girls who were playing near the rock. Suddenly, a group of large hungry bears appeared. The girls ran as fast as they could to escape the bears. They came upon a wide rock and climbed onto it. The girls prayed to the rock to save them. It began to rise into the air, pushing them into the sky.

The Lakota Indians had a spooky name for this great rock formation: Ghost Mountain.

FRIGHTENING OR FUN?

The Kiowa legend says that the bears' claw marks can still be seen on the sides of Devils Tower.

SACRED SPACE

More than 20 other Native American tribes have stories about Devils Tower, including the Cheyenne, Crow, and Arapaho. This tells us how holy, or sacred, the formation was to native peoples.

The Lakota used the tower for **funerals**, healings, and other **ceremonies**. Small huts have been found near the tower. People probably used them for prayer. Lakota still perform the Sun Dance at Devils Tower. This ceremony is meant to take away the world's pain and heal nature.

FRIGHTENING OR FUN?

Devils Tower was the landing place of aliens in a 1977 movie called *Close Encounters of the Third Kind.*

Signs and prayer flags remind visitors of Devils Tower's special place in Native American society.

THE TOWER IS HELD SACRED BY MANY AMERICAN INDIANS AND HIGHLY REGARDED BY OTHER PEOPLES. RESPECT THIS PLACE BY STAYING ON TRAILS

REMARKABLE PEAK

European explorers of America may have seen Devils Tower, but none noted it in their writings. One group reported being chased away by unfriendly Indians in the nearby Black Hills.

Devils Tower wasn't given its American name until a **US Geological Survey** saw it in 1875. Colonel Richard Dodge called it "one of the most remarkable **peaks** in this or any country." He's given credit for naming it. One of his men mistakenly thought the Indians called it "the bad god's tower." So, Dodge named it "the devil's tower."

The name of Devils Tower may have been a mistake, but it can still look spooky rising above the plains at night.

HOT ROCK

How can a rock just rise above the rest of the land as Devils Tower does? The makeup of Devils Tower gives us a clue about how it formed. It's made of igneous rock. Igneous rock forms from the hot, liquid rock within Earth called magma.

Most geologists think that, about 65 million years ago, magma pushed itself near Earth's surface and cooled. Over millions of years, the land around the cooled rock **eroded**, leaving Devils Tower standing tall. Devils Tower is known as an igneous **intrusion**.

FRIGHTENING OR FUN?

Magma can be hotter than
2,300°F (1,260°C).

The magma that formed Devils Tower
cooled into six-sided shapes, or hexagons.

A TOWERING HOME

Devils Tower might look just like a giant rock, but it's actually a home for many kinds of plants and animals. **Lichen** covers parts of the rock, and moss and grass grow on top.

Numerous kinds of birds live and raise families near or on Devils Tower. They include great blue herons, turkey vultures, red-tailed hawks, and red-headed woodpeckers. Chipmunks live on top of Devils Tower, and many black-tailed prairie dogs live near the base, too!

lichen

A group of prairie dog families that live together is called a town. There aren't as many prairie dog towns as there once were. The land around Devils Tower provides a good home for these animals.

TAKING CARE OF THE TOWER

The US government knew that Devils Tower was very special. It wanted to do something to keep it safe from people who wanted to buy it and keep it for themselves. The Antiquities Act of 1906 was the first American law to help guard **natural resources**. It allowed the president to set aside "objects of historic or scientific interest."

Under this law, Devils Tower was named the first US national **monument** on September 24, 1906, by President Theodore Roosevelt.

Devils Tower was once "Devil's Tower," *with* an apostrophe. However, the paper that President Roosevelt signed making it a national monument spelled it *without* the apostrophe—Devils Tower. That name stuck!

NATIONAL PARK SERVICE

Devils Tower National Monument

National Park Service
U.S. Department of the Interior

1906-20__
CENT____

17

A LONG WAY UP!

If you want a really scary experience, try climbing Devils Tower! One of the men in the US Geological Survey of 1875 said the top of Devils Tower was **"inaccessible to anything without wings."** He thought no one could ever climb it. Yet, people have been climbing Devils Tower for more than 100 years!

Most climbers free climb, which means they use cracks and shelves in the rock to pull themselves up. Some use climbing tools, though. Ropes and **harnesses** are used for extra safety.

FRIGHTENING OR FUN?

In 1941, a man **parachuted** to the top of Devils Tower. However, he couldn't climb down. He had to wait 6 days for someone to rescue him!

The Devils Tower park service asks climbers not to climb the rock in the month of June because some Indian tribes still have ceremonies during that month.

19

DISAPPEARING?

Devils Tower is slowly eroding. Wind and rain break off pieces. In fact, the base of the monument is littered with scree, which is the name for rock piles at the base of a cliff, hill, or mountain.

You don't have to worry, though. It took 65 million years for Devils Tower to form, and it'll take a very, very long time for it to disappear! That's good news for animals and plants that live on the monument and for the many people who visit this amazing place each year.

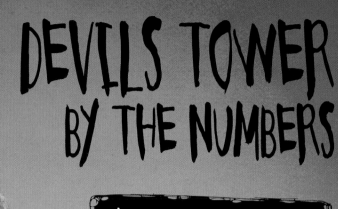

DEVILS TOWER
BY THE NUMBERS

became a national monument: 1906

height from base to summit: 867 feet (264 m)

distance around base: 1 mile (1.6 km)

average time to climb: 5 hours

fastest climb: 18 minutes

More than 450,000 people
visit Devils Tower each year.

GLOSSARY

ceremony: an event to honor or celebrate something

erode: to wear away outer layers of rock or soil by the action of wind and water

funeral: a ceremony to mark the burial of the dead

harness: a set of straps fitted to a person to keep them in place

inaccessible: hard or impossible to reach

intrusion: a body of igneous rock that has moved into spaces in older, solid rock

legend: a story that has been passed down for many, many years that's unlikely to be true

lichen: a gray, green, or yellow plantlike organism made up of a fungus and an alga, and often appearing in flat patches on rocks

monument: a place or structure set aside or kept safe because of its importance

natural resource: something in nature that can be used by people

parachute: to use a specially shaped piece of cloth that collects air to slow down when falling

peak: the top of a mountain

US Geological Survey: the US government science agency that studies the nation's land and resources

FOR MORE INFORMATION

Books

Britton, Tamara L. *Devils Tower*. Edina, MN: ABDO Publishing, 2005.

Petersen, Christine. *Rockin' Rocks*. Edina, MN: ABDO Publishing, 2010.

Weil, Ann. *The World's Most Amazing Monuments*. Chicago, IL: Raintree, 2012.

Websites

Devils Tower
www.nps.gov/deto/
Learn all you need to know about Devils Tower's history and what you can expect when you visit.

Devils Tower
education.nationalgeographic.com/education/media/devils-tower-geology/?ar_a=1
Find out more about how Devils Tower formed.

INDEX